My **BED**
and Other Home Furniture

Helen Greathead

W9-BUI-501

CRABTREE
Publishing Company
www.crabtreebooks.com

Crabtree Publishing Company
www.crabtreebooks.com
1-800-387-7650

Published in Canada
Crabtree Publishing
616 Welland Avenue
St. Catharines, ON
L2M 5V6

Published in the United States
Crabtree Publishing
PMB 59051
350 Fifth Ave, 59th Floor
New York, NY 10118

Author: Helen Greathead

Editorial director: Kathy Middleton

Editors: Julia Bird and Ellen Rodger

Designer: Q2A Media

Proofreader: Wendy Scavuzzo

Prepress technician: Margaret Amy Salter

Print and production coordinator: Katherine Berti

Published by Crabtree Publishing Company in 2017

First published in 2015 by Franklin Watts
(A division of Hachette Children's Books)
Copyright © Franklin Watts 2015

Printed in Canada/072016/PB20160525

Photographs:
Front Cover: Pinkcandy, Ewa Studio, Robert_s, Chen ws, Holbox, Graphixmania/ Shutterstock. Back Cover: Iriana Shiyan/Shutterstock. Title Page: Baker Alhashki, Ksenia Palimski, PzAxe, Graphixmania, Chukcha, Getideaka, Viphotos, Ozaiachin/ Shutterstock. Imprint Page: Syda Productions/Shutterstock. P4: Semarang Suite; P5(T): Leonid Ikan/Shutterstock, P5(B): Ekler/Shutterstock; P6–7(BKGRD): K. Miri Photography/Shutterstock, P6: K. Miri Photography/Shutterstock; P7(T): TongChuwit/Shutterstock, P7(BR): Sasimoto/Shutterstock, P7(BL): David Selman/ Cardinal/Corbis; P8–9(BKGRD): K. Miri Photography/Shutterstock, P8(B): White Lotus, P8(T): Frank Polich/Reuters; P9(B): Leslye Davis/The New York Times/Redux Pictures; P10–11(BKGRD): Ti Santi/Shutterstock, P10(B): Monkey Business Images/ Shutterstock; P11(B): Thor Jorgen Udvang/Shutterstock, P11(T): Andrew Rowat/Getty Images; P12: Lou Linwei/Alamy, P12–13(BKGRD): Ti Santi/Shutterstock, P13(T): Kisno Weaver (INORI)/ Fairtrade Furniture, P13(B): Ruzpage/Shutterstock; P14–15(BKGRD): Tom Gowanlock/Shutterstock, P14(B): Nikolpetr/Shutterstock, P15(T): D 200 Collection/Balan Madhavan/Alamy, P15(C): FLPA /Alamy, P15(B): Picsfive/ Shutterstock; P16(L): Picsfive/Shutterstock, P16(BR): Fabien Monteil/Shutterstock, P16(TR):Studio Swine; P17(T): Tom Gowanlock/Shutterstock, P17(B): Anna Beruad/Malika org; P18: wavebreakmedia/Shutterstock, P19(B): Hector Conesa/ Shutterstock, P19(T): Lisette Van Der Hoorn/Shutterstock; P20(T):Forest Stewardship Council, P20(B): Guentermanaus/Shutterstock; P21(T): TongChuwit/Shutterstock, P21(C): Siiren, P21(B): Sneh Gupta 2014; P22-23(BKGRD): Fredredhat/Shutterstock, P22(CL):IlyaAkinshin/Shutterstock, P22(CR):Ilya Akinshin/Shutterstock, P22(C): Andresr/Shutterstock; P23(C): Alan Bailey/Shutterstock, P23(T):Ilya Akinshin/ Shutterstock; P24(TL):Ilya Akinshin/Shutterstock, P24(TR): TongChuwit/Shutterstock, P24(B): Sue Smith/Shutterstock, P24(C): Ross Parry Picture Agency; P25(T): Akintunde Akinleye/Reuters, P25(B): Friedrich Stark/Alamy, P26(CR): FedeCandoniPhoto/ Shutterstock, P26(CL):Ahmad Faizal Yahya/Shutterstock, P26–27(BKGRD): Maffi/ Shutterstock, P27(BL):Ten Thousand Villages, P27(BC):Ten Thousand Villages, P27(T): Goodweave.org, P27(BR):Ahmad Faizal Yahya/Shutterstock; P28–29(BKGRD): Maffi/ Shutterstock, P28(T): Goodweave.org, P28(B): Goodweave.org; P29(BR): Designboom, P29(BL): MadeByNode; P30–31: Andresr, Fabien Monteil, Hector Conesa, Monkey Business Images, Ruzpage; Ahmad Faizal Yahya, Nikolpetr,FedeCandoniPhoto,Leon id Ikan, Wavebreakmedia, K. Miri Photography/Shutterstock;D 200 Collection/Balan Madhavan/Alamy; Semarang suite; Kisno weaver (INORI)/Fairtrade Furniture; Lou Linwei/Alamy; P32(T): Fabien Monteil/Shutterstock. Illustrations: all-free-downloads. com: (4–5, 18–19, 19–20)

Library and Archives Canada Cataloguing in Publication

Greathead, Helen, author
　　My bed and other home furniture / Helen Greathead.

(Well made, fair trade)
Includes index.
Issued in print and electronic formats.
ISBN 978-0-7787-2713-2 (hardback).--
ISBN 978-0-7787-2717-0 (paperback).--
ISBN 978-1-4271-1843-1 (html)

　　1. Furniture industry and trade--Juvenile literature. 2. Furniture industry and trade--Moral and ethical aspects--Juvenile literature. 3. Furniture workers--Juvenile literature. I. Title.

HD9773.A2G74 2016　　　　j381'.456841　　　C2016-902568-3
　　　　　　　　　　　　　　　　　　　　　　　　　　　　　　　C2016-902569-1

Library of Congress Cataloging-in-Publication Data

Names: Greathead, Helen, author.
Title: My bed and other home furniture / Helen Greathead.
Description: New York : Crabtree Publishing, 2017. |
　　Series: Well made, fair trade | Audience: Grade 7 to 8. |
　　Audience: Age: 10-14+ | Includes index.
Identifiers: LCCN 2016016657 (print) | LCCN 2016027399 (ebook) |
　　ISBN 9780778727132 (reinforced library binding) |
　　ISBN 9780778727170 (pbk.) |
　　ISBN 9781427118431 (electronic HTML)
Subjects: LCSH: Furniture industry and trade--Juvenile literature.
Classification: LCC HD9773.A2 G74 2017 (print) |
　　LCC HD9773.A2 (ebook) | DDC 338.4/76841--dc23
LC record available at https://lccn.loc.gov/2016016657

OCT   2016

Contents

Words in **bold** can be found in the glossary on page 30.

Fair trade furniture

Furniture is big business. Today, many companies are starting to look at how furniture can be made in a way that is fair to workers and safe for the environment.

Why buy fair trade?

Around the world, many problems are caused through furniture production. Workers are often poorly paid and endure poor working conditions, such as health and safety dangers from the chemicals they use in glue or paint. The World Fair Trade Organization (WFTO) is an international group that believes in fair trade practices. Companies who belong to the WFTO pay their workers fairly, help to care for local **communities**, and make sure that nothing they do damages wildlife or the environment.

The Fair Trade Furniture Company is a member of the WFTO. Its furniture is made in Indonesia using natural materials. The company's workers are paid a fair wage, and have health and education programs.

What is best to buy?

When buying new furniture, it is important to know what it is made of and where it has come from. This is known as the **supply chain**. When your family is buying a new item of furniture, look carefully at any labels or logos. Does it have a WFTO label or a Forest Stewardship Council (FSC) logo? The FSC is an American company that makes sure trees used to make furniture have come from forests that are well-managed and **sustainable** (see page 20).

The FSC protects the world's forests, as well as local communities and wildlife.

What can I do?

This book will explain how fair trade programs help workers to make a decent living, improve working conditions, and protect the environment and wildlife. It will give you ideas about what you can do to help when choosing furniture with your family, and how to recycle old or unwanted furniture.

This map shows the places mentioned in the book that are involved in fair trade projects.

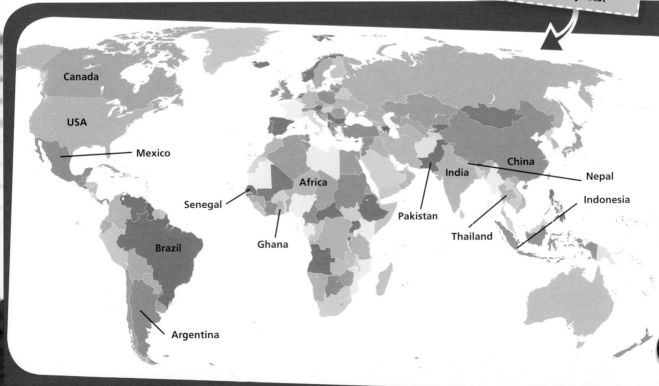

Canada

USA

Mexico

Brazil

Argentina

Senegal

Ghana

Africa

India

Pakistan

Thailand

China

Nepal

Indonesia

Beds and mattresses

The first mattresses were made of straw, leaves, and even animal skins. Today, mattresses contain many different parts.

How are mattresses made?

Mattresses with springs started being made in the mid-1700s. Today, the inside of a spring mattress has anywhere from 250 to 1,000 connecting springs, and at least five layers of cushioning around them. Some parts of the mattress are made by hand. The quilted fabric cover is stitched using a giant quilting machine, then cut to the correct size and added to the mattress.

The quilted padding that covers the top, bottom, and sides of most mattresses is made by machines in factories.

Where are beds and mattresses made?

Beds and mattresses are manufactured all over the world, with China and the United States being the main producers. China and Poland **export** more mattresses than any other countries. The Sealy Mattress Company is the world's largest manufacturer of beds and mattresses. The main company is based in Ohio, but it is represented in many other countries, including Canada, Saudi Arabia, Japan, Australia, and Argentina.

Most bed and mattress companies get their materials from all around the world. For example, the Turkish company Boycelik manufactures mattress springs made from carbon steel wire which comes from Europe and Turkey. The company exports its finished springs to 65 countries around the world.

Reuse, recycle

Today, 90 percent of beds and mattresses can be recycled. Metal from the mattress springs can be melted down and reused. Wooden bed frames can be broken up and used for garden **mulch**. Paper, plastic, and fabrics can be used for building **insulation**.

Getting rid of old mattresses can be a problem. Millions used to end up in garbage dumps.

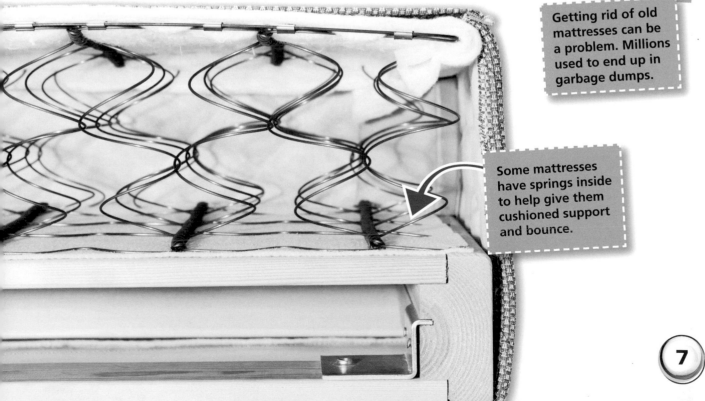

Some mattresses have springs inside to help give them cushioned support and bounce.

Mattresses and cushions are often treated with **toxic** glues and **flame retardants**. These coatings can damage the health of the people who make mattresses and cushions, because they inhale toxic fumes that can make them ill. Workers need protection from glue and other sprays, and should work in spaces that are well **ventilated**.

Sleep safe

Sometimes flame retardants are mixed with the foam that is produced for use in mattresses. Sleeping on these foam mattresses can cause an allergic reaction, such as swollen eyes or lips, rashes, and difficulty breathing. Natural **latex** is a safe alternative.

This mattress is being tested to see if it contains enough flame retardant. In the U.S., the law requires a mattress to be able to withstand a 2-foot (60 cm)wide blowtorch flame for 70 seconds.

Best buy!

White Lotus in New Jersey produces mattresses using natural materials and no chemicals. Instead of springs, the core of the mattress is made from natural latex, a plant-based material that is **biodegradable**. White Lotus mattresses do not need to be treated with dangerous flame retardants, as the outer layer of organic wool padding is naturally fireproof.

The latex core of this White Lotus mattress is wrapped in 100 percent New Zealand wool and 100 percent organic cotton.

Case study: Taylorsville furniture factory, North Carolina

In 2010, Sheri Farley was working in a furniture factory in Taylorsville, North Carolina. Factory workers were paid $9 an hour to glue **polyurethane** foam to chairs, sofas, and mattresses. The work involved standing all day and using a spray gun to apply the glue. The pay was reasonable, but it hardly made up for the illness Sheri now suffers.

Better place to work

Sheri was employed at the factory for five years, but today she is no longer well enough to work. It is likely that a chemical (n-propyl bromide, or nPB) in the glue damaged nerve endings in Sheri's body, causing severe pain along her spine and in her legs. One in seven people suffers after working with the glue, and the effects can show up in just two weeks. Facemasks and proper ventilation in the workplace could have solved the problem.

Following United States government research and tests, the glue was given a hazard warning in 2013. Employers are now expected to:
- limit the amount of time employees spend using the glue in the workplace
- provide breathing masks and clothing for their staff
- train employees to use the glue safely.

Sheri Farley walks with a limp and uses a stick for support. She finds it difficult to balance and is frequently in pain.

Armchairs and sofas

Your sofa is probably one of the most expensive pieces of furniture in your home. That is because it takes time, care, and special knowledge to make.

How are sofas and chairs made?

It can take up to 600 hours to make a top-quality sofa, and most of the work has to be done by hand. First, the wooden frame is built, then strips of **webbing** are added to hold the seat in place. Springs may be attached to the webbing with **twine**. The padding, which is added to each section separately, might be made from horsehair, foam, or **polyester**. It is sewn into place and held in position with fabric coverings. The panels for the outer cover are cut, stapled, or sewn on, then cushions are added.

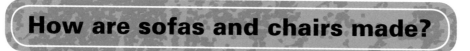

Soft armchairs and sofas can contain up to 1,000 tacks, 590 feet (180 m) of twine, and hundreds of feet of sewing thread.

Where are sofas and chairs made?

Traditionally, Italy was the top producer of quality leather sofas. In 1998, one Italian company started producing its sofas in China. The Chinese workers were paid less and worked longer hours, so the furniture made there was much cheaper to produce. Many U.S. companies have also moved their factories to China. Several different types and brands of chairs and sofas are now made there, as well as other kinds of furniture.

Workers in a Chinese furniture factory cut and style leather and fur material to cover chairs and sofas.

Low pay, long hours

Working in Chinese furniture factories can be tough, with long hours and low pay. Factories may be overcrowded and unsafe, with workers offered little protection from cutting equipment or paint and varnish fumes. Young Chinese people today have better education than their parents and want better opportunities. As a result, factory owners are starting to improve working conditions and offer salaries above the minimum wage.

This worker sprays varnish on furniture in a production line in China.

Case study: China's furniture factories

In 2005, 300,000 furniture jobs were lost in the United States and moved to China. While American workers could earn over $15 an hour, the same jobs in China in 2008 paid just 70 cents an hour. In 2008, 25-year-old Zhao Xia worked in a factory preparing furniture to be painted. She had only two days off each month and regularly worked until midnight. She lived with her husband in a small room near the factory. Zhao Xia put up with these conditions rather than work in the fields all day. Today, workers' attitudes have begun to change.

Factory workers sewing upholstery for furniture in Guangdong, southern China.

Better place to work

Circle Furniture, based in Shenzhen, China, manufactures living room suites and a wide range of other furniture. Bruce Lee, the owner of the company, understands that to keep good workers he has to be a fair employer. The company now provides food and accommodations where workers can live with their families. Some workers are even given a free motor scooter to use for their journey to and from the factory. With young workers becoming increasingly unhappy about factory pay and working conditions, perhaps more employers will follow Circle Furniture's example in the future.

Renewable rattan

Rattan looks like bamboo and grows in areas with tropical rain forests, such as Indonesia. Rattan has become popular for use in fair trade furniture because it is easier to cut down and transport than **timber**, and it grows back much faster. It is also light, tough, and flexible, making it the perfect sustainable material.

Best buy!

Inori is an agency that helps small producers of traditionally made Indonesian chairs find fair trade buyers. They work with Kisno, a small family workshop, and Mandiri Craft, which trains disabled people to make seat frames and other wooden furniture parts. Mandiri Craft employs up to 50 workers who might otherwise have no work because of their disabilities.

Kisno furniture is woven by hand according to local Indonesian skills and traditions.

About 80 percent of the world's raw rattan products come from Indonesia. Rattan is bendable and can be woven to make furniture, pots, and baskets.

Plastic furniture

Plastic furniture is cheap, lightweight, and useful. However, the making and disposing of it is having a negative impact on the environment.

How is plastic furniture made?

Plastic furniture was first introduced at the end of the 1940s because of a demand for low-cost home furnishings. Today, the cheapest plastic furniture is made using injection molding. This process involves a shaped metal mold that is filled with **polypropylene** that has been heated to a specific temperature. The mold cools down and a solid plastic piece of furniture is removed. This is called monobloc furniture because it is made in one piece.

Due to **mass production,** plastic chairs and tables are very cheap and are now seen everywhere. Plastic furniture is especially popular for use outdoors in gardens.

Mass production

Today, mass production can turn out hundreds of thousands of monobloc chairs each year. At first, production was limited to France and the United States, but now the chairs are also made in Russia, Taiwan, Australia, Mexico, Europe, Turkey, Israel, and China. It is estimated that one monobloc chair is made every minute.

This factory in India produces plastic furniture, including monobloc chairs.

What is wrong with plastic?

Plastic is made from oil and gas, which are **fossil fuels** that are not renewable. Making plastic furniture uses up to 4 percent of all the oil and gas that is produced each year, and a further 3 to 4 percent is used to manufacture the furniture itself. Plastic furniture may be light and easy to use, but it also takes thousands of years to break down. In Europe, 50 percent of plastic waste, including furniture, still goes to the dump.

Plastic chairs, such as this red one, are cheap to buy so people often don't think twice about throwing them away. Millions of chairs end up in garbage dumps.

Floating on the ocean

An estimated 100,000 tons of plastic waste, such as bags, bottles, and even furniture, has made its way into the oceans. The plastic breaks down into **microplastics**, which are easily swallowed. Many animals and birds are killed or injured as a result. Chemical additives from the plastics can also get into the **food chain**. Fish eat the microplastics, then the fish are eaten by humans and other animals.

Responsible waste

Plastic furniture doesn't have to go to waste. It can easily be recycled by businesses and individual consumers through local recycling programs. In 2012 in the United States, more than 1,800 companies specialized in the disposal of all types of plastic waste, but only about 10 percent of discarded plastics were disposed of responsibly.

Every year, thousands of tons of plastic waste wash up on beaches around the world. This causes pollution and is dangerous to people and wildlife.

Best buy!

An island of plastic that is twice the size of the United States floats on the Pacific Ocean, and it is getting bigger. This stool, from the Sea Chair Project, was made by design students who are worried about ocean pollution. The chair is made entirely from plastic reclaimed from the ocean.

Each item made for the Sea Chair Project has a tag with its production number and other data to show where the plastic came from.

Case study: Recycled plastics, Senegal, West Africa

In Senegal, West Africa, plastic pollution in the city of Thiès was so bad that the local people approached an Italian waste management organization for help. By 2002, their region had two plastic recycling centers. Plastic is brought to the centers—sometimes by donkey and cart—to be sorted into color and type, then washed. Creating enough heat to melt the plastic uses too much electricity and causes carbon dioxide **emissions** that harm the atmosphere. Instead, the plastic is cut by hand into small pieces, then ground into pellets or powders by a machine.

Jobs and training

The recycling centers create jobs for local people and provide training in management, accounting, and machine operation. Adult reading and writing classes are also offered. By 2008, one center had recycled 150 tons of plastic, and prevented an estimated 273 tons of carbon dioxide emissions.

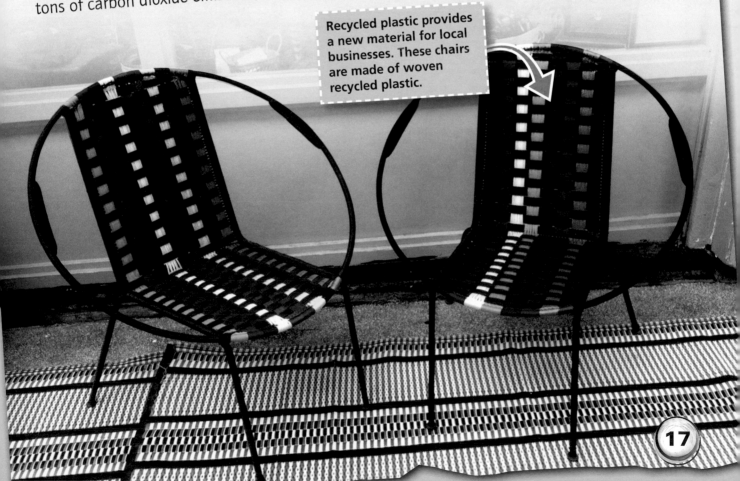

Recycled plastic provides a new material for local businesses. These chairs are made of woven recycled plastic.

Wooden furniture

The demand for furniture made from wood is growing. This means forests around the world are being destroyed, which is causing problems.

A wooden table is long-lasting, but the wood may not have come from a sustainable forest.

How are tables made?

Tables have been used for centuries. Today, most are made from wood and held together by glue and screws. The wood is stored at 50-84 °F (10–29 °C) so it does not shrink or expand. The planks are glued together to form the tabletop and clamped together while the glue dries. Then the top is sanded down and cut to shape. The legs are shaped on a machine called a profiler. The table is assembled, then it is stained, sealed, sanded, and **lacquered** by hand.

Where does the wood come from?

Some wood for furniture comes from tropical rain forests, while other types come from sustainable forests that are grown specifically for making furniture. Asian countries, such as China, India, Vietnam, Indonesia, and Malaysia, produce a huge amount of timber. India has some of the largest rain forests in the world, and 93 percent of its furniture exports are made from wood.

Large areas of rain forest are disappearing every day through **logging** to produce timber for furniture. The loss of rain forest has a devastating effect on the environment and local people.

Millions of trees are cut down and turned into logs to be made into furniture. This means rain forests around the world are shrinking.

In Cameroon, West Africa, the Baka people use rain forest trees and plants for vital medicines. But in southeast Cameroon, nearly all Baka land has been lost to loggers.

Climate change

Trees absorb carbon dioxide. When a rain forest is cut down, the loss of trees results in more carbon dioxide in the atmosphere, which increases **climate change**. As well, the cleared land dries out very quickly because it is no longer sheltered from the sun. This causes the plants and wildlife in the area to die.

Deforestation in the Amazon, the world's biggest rain forest. Over 440 new species of animals and plants have been discovered in this forest over the past four years. It is estimated 150 acres (60.7 hectares) of rain forest around the world are burned every minute.

Sustaining the forests

At the current rate of **deforestation**, it is estimated that in 100 years there will be no rain forests left. Many organizations, such as the Forest Stewardship Council (FSC), have programs around the world to protect the world's rain forests. These programs promote environmentally responsible forest management, which includes cutting down trees at a sustainable rate, fair employment standards, and protection of wildlife.

Look for the FSC logo on wood or paper items you buy.

Special policy

Kingfisher is Europe's largest home-improvement company, with more than 1,000 stores in nine countries. One third of Kingfisher's products are made from timber. Eighty-nine percent of the wood they use is sustainable, and Kingfisher hopes to use 100 percent sustainable wood by 2020. To improve sustainability, they are starting to enlarge some of the forests in the countries where the company is based. By 2050, they hope to create more forest than they need to use for products, leaving the unused forest as a habitat for wildlife.

Case study: Myakka fair trade company

All furniture produced by Myakka, a company in the United Kingdom, is fair trade and made in India, Indonesia, and Thailand. The company uses sustainable **hardwoods** from **certified suppliers**, and helps fund replanting programs in Indonesia. Buying directly from the furniture manufacturer keeps Myakka's supply chain short, and payment to the producers high. They pay a fair price, which means better conditions for workers and benefits for their families, too. One small producer has now bought the land its workshops are built on.

School for disabled children

Myakka also supports SKSN, a boarding school for disabled children in Rajasthan, India. There, more than 500 disabled children learn skills that will help them find work. Donations from Myakka support the school's career training center, where some of Myakka's products are made.

Reuse, recycle

This brightly colored table by Budi uses recycled wood.

This wood table is made from recycled Indonesian fishing boats. Bali artist Budi sells all his furniture through a fair trade exporter called Siiren. He gets a fair price for his work and Siiren makes sure that all their craftspeople benefit from good working conditions.

Raj Kanwar lost the use of her legs at the age of two. The training she receives at SKSN gives her hope that, despite her disability, she will develop the skills to find work in the future.

Refrigerators

Fridges enable people to keep food fresh for quite a while, but some of the chemicals fridges contain can cause serious damage to the environment if they are not disposed of properly.

The energy we waste keeping the fridge door open each year could run a dishwasher 20 times.

What are refrigerators made from?

The earliest fridges were holes in the ground, lined with straw or wood and packed with ice or snow. Today's refrigerators usually have a steel casing, with vacuum-formed plastic on the inside. The space between the inside and outside of the fridge is filled with foam, to keep the inner shell cool. Tubes filled with a cooling substance pass from a **condenser** at the bottom of the fridge and around the inside, keeping the contents at 41°F (5°C) or below, which slows the growth of **bacteria** in food.

Where are fridges made?

In 1834, Jacob Perkins of Massachusetts made the first working refrigeration machine. Fridges quickly became popular, and refrigerators are now produced all over the world. Many fridge factories in developing countries such as Brazil and India pay workers poorly for long working hours in unsafe conditions.

Case study: Whirlpool Corporation, Brazil

In Argentina, Brazil, India, and Mexico, the American company Whirlpool has been voted one of the best places to work. Whirlpool believes that employees must work in a healthy and safe environment, be treated with respect, and be paid at least the minimum amount recommended by local laws for all hours worked. The company also ensures its employees do not work more than 60 hours a week.

Work for women

Whirlpool runs a variety of community projects, such as a program to improve employment opportunities for women in Brazil. The program helps young single mothers who may have difficulty finding work, as well as older women who may have never learned to read or write. Business **cooperatives** sponsored by the program provide workshops, classes, and educational support, which help the women's employment prospects.

Whirlpool offers classes in workplace skills, such as computing.

Getting rid of old fridges

Older fridge models use up to three times the electricity of newer models, and they may contain chemicals that are now banned, such as **CFCs**, which are dangerous to humans and harmful to the **ozone layer**. Discarded fridges can cause many problems. Some are shipped to developing countries such as Ghana, where they may be bought cheaply for use in homes, or dumped on illegal scrap heaps. Local people, including children, make money by taking the used fridges apart and selling any materials they can.

The chemicals inside fridges and freezers can leak when fridges are dumped. This is dangerous for people and the environment.

Reuse, recycle

Emily Cummins designed a solar fridge when she was just 16 years old. The solar fridge uses two cylinders, one sitting inside the other, and can be made from scrap materials such as old car parts. The space between the two cylinders is filled with sand, wool, or soil, then soaked with water. In the heat of the Sun, the water evaporates, keeping the contents of the inner cylinder at a temperature of 42 °F (6 °C). The food inside the fridge is kept cool and dry at all times.

Sustainable fridges designed by Emily Cummins are now used in Zambia, Namibia, and South Africa.

Case study: Agbogbloshie, Accra, Ghana

Agbogbloshie is a poor town with a scrap heap on the outskirts of Ghana's capital city, Accra. There, local people take fridges apart, sell what they don't need, and keep the metal. The metal is cut and hammered into cooking pots, or head pans, which construction workers use for carrying concrete on their heads. Each pan sells for just over $3.

Banned shipments

Ghana banned shipments of second-hand fridges in January 2013 because of environmental concerns, but at the end of the year some were still arriving. The government of Ghana now plans to offer discounts on new fridges to stop the trade in second-hand appliances, and hopes to create more and safer jobs by manufacturing them locally.

A head pan being used on a construction site in Nigeria.

Young men in Ghana breaking up old refrigerators. One old fridge will make up to 10 cooking pots.

Carpets and rugs

Carpets can be both beautiful and practical, whether they are made in a modern factory or produced by hand following age-old traditions.

Carpets are made all over the world, from the United States to China. Persian carpets (from Iran) are well known for their high quality, and date back 2,500 years.

How are carpets made?

To produce a **tufted** carpet, strips of yarn are spun together. The yarn is stitched onto backing material. Patterns and colors are added, the pieces of carpet are stitched together, and the back is coated with latex. The carpet is steamed, brushed, vacuumed, and trimmed before it is rolled into a tube and ready to be sold.

Child labor

In some parts of South Asia, children aged 7 to 14 are employed to make rugs and carpets, often to pay off a family debt. The children receive very low pay, or become unpaid slaves in the industry. They work long hours in cramped, dark conditions, often without enough food. Their eyesight, growth, and breathing (through inhaling fine wool fibers) can all be harmed. The sharp tools they use can also cause injuries.

GoodWeave was set up in 1994 by Kailash Satyarthi, an Indian children's **rights activist**. The group is made up of charities and non-profit organizations. It has been working to end illegal child labor in South Asia, and inspects carpet factories to free child workers and help them get an education.

Carpets carrying the GoodWeave symbol show that they do not use child labor. Profits help to fund factory inspections and educate freed child workers.

Best buy!

Bunyaad is a group based around Lahore, Pakistan. It sells beautiful hand-crafted rugs in Canada and the United States. Bunyaad started work in the 1960s to help keep jobs and the age-old rug-making traditions alive in small villages. Today, Bunyaad works with about 850 families in 100 villages. The workers are paid a fair wage and extra fair trade income might buy a water buffalo, for example, to provide yogurt and butter, which are essential to Pakistani cooking.

These all-wool rugs made by workers from Bunyaad are hand-spun, using only natural dyes. They take 10 to 12 months to make.

Case study: Kathmandu, Nepal

Sanju lives in Kathmandu and is one of tens of thousands of children known as "carpet kids" throughout South Asia. At 11 years old, she was sent to work in a carpet factory by her family because they could not afford to take care of her. Young children are used to make carpets because their small fingers are good for knotting handmade carpets. Sanju was never paid, worked from 4:00 a.m. until 8:00 p.m., had no time off, and was always hungry. She cried every day.

A better life

Sanju thought things would never change, but one day an inspector from GoodWeave visited the factory, and helped to get her and other children to their **rehabilitation** center. Now Sanju is back living with her family, going to school, and playing sports. She is also helping to teach the other young girls that come to the center.

In this painting, Sanju has shown herself without arms (right) because she felt trapped and very unhappy. Then she appears on the left with her arms outspread to show how happy and free she feels.

Thanks to the education provided by GoodWeave, Sanju now believes she has a much brighter future. She is learning to enjoy herself and have fun!

Untouchables

Kumbeshwar Technical School (KTS) began as a project to help people in Nepal who are labeled "untouchable," meaning people in the lowest **caste** or social system. Untouchables could only work in certain jobs, such as cleaning the streets and sewers, in exchange for scraps of food. The Kumbeshwar project began in 1983 with a childcare program and a literacy course for adults. The adults were then trained in knitting and carpet weaving and, by 1985, they began selling their wares. By selling through fair trade organizations, such as Node, the project is also able to fund an orphanage and a primary school. In 2013, some Node rugs were even exhibited in London's Design Museum.

Best buy!

Node is a not-for-profit business that creates fair trade rugs using designs by illustrators and designers from around the world. You can even design your own! The carpets are made by hand, using pure Tibetan wool, dyed with natural dyes that do not harm the environment, and knotted onto looms, or weaving frames, by hand.

Node rug makers are founding members of Fair Trade Nepal. Workers receive fair wages and the company supports a school of 260 children, as well as an orphanage.

This suitcase used to be a carpet! Recycled carpets mixed with **resin** from rapeseed oil make up the case's hard shell.

Environment matters

Today, you can buy carpets with reduced or recycled yarn or recycled backing material. Installing carpets without glue, and using carpet tiles (so you only replace areas that are worn) also helps make new carpets more environmentally friendly. At the end of its life, a carpet can be recycled.

Glossary

bacteria Tiny, single-celled living things that are found everywhere; some cause diseases

biodegradable Can be broken down without causing pollution

caste A system of social status in Hinduism

certified suppliers People in the supply chain who have been inspected and approved for following regulations

CFC Chlorofluorocarbons, gases that are harmful to the ozone layer

climate change A process in which the environment changes to become warmer, colder, drier, or wetter than normal

cooperative A group of people or organizations working together

communities Groups of people who live and work closely together

condenser Series of copper tubes inside a fridge that help transfer heat from the inside of the fridge to the outside

deforestation Cutting down trees without planting new trees to replace them

emissions Release or discharge substances, such as gases

export To sell goods outside of the country where they were made

flame retardant A substance applied to fabric, wood, or other material to make it resistant to catching fire

food chain A chain of living things in which each member uses the member below as food

fossil fuels Natural materials such as oil or coal which come from Earth

hardwoods Wood from trees that produce seeds which are covered by some sort of fruit or shell

insulation Material used as a protective layer

lacquered Painted with a shiny finish

latex A type of rubber made from the sap of a rubber tree

logging Chopping down trees and preparing them to be cut into wood for building

mass production Making a huge amount of the same thing by machine

microplastics Tiny pieces or particles of plastic smaller than 0.4 inches (1 mm)

mulch A covering of rotting vegetable matter or leaves that is spread over soil to protect plants or help them grow

ozone layer The layer around Earth's atmosphere that protects it from ultra-violet rays from the Sun

polyester A fabric made from synthetic fiber

polyurethane A chemical material used in paint and varnish

polypropylene A chemical resin used as a molding material

rattan A climbing plant that grows up trees in tropical rain forests

rehabilitation Helping people to get well and rebuild their lives

resin A sticky liquid that oozes from some trees and plants

rights activist A person who is very active in fighting for the rights of other people, animals, or the environment

supply chain The order of how materials or goods are obtained and put together to produce a finished product

sustainable Able to be used without being completely used up or destroyed

timber Wood from trees

toxic Poisonous or harmful

tufted Where yarn for a carpet is inserted into a ready woven backing, which is then stuck to another backing material

twine A strong string

ventilated Has a supply of fresh air

webbing Strong, narrow fabric used in chairs to make a base for chair seats

Websites

Visit these fair trade websites to find out more about fair trade and the products you can buy:
www.fairtradeusa.org
www.cftn.ca

Find out more about the Sea Chair Project and the dangers of plastic waste in our oceans:
http://www.studioswine.com/sea-chair

See what else can be done with an old fishing boat here: **http://.balirecycledboat.com/** and here: **http://www.siiren.co.uk/departments-c334/ethnic-rustic-furniture-c265/hand-carved-solid-wooden-recycled-boat-table-p1497**

See more of Emily Cummins's inventions here: **www.emilycummins.co.uk/about**

Read the stories of some of the children who have been freed from working in the carpet industry: **www.goodweave.org/children_stories**

See some fabulous Node rug designs and a video that shows how they are made here: **www.madebynode.com/**

Check out what the Fair Trade Furniture Company has to say about protecting the environment: **http://fairtradefurniture.co.uk/modern-conservatory-furniture/environment/**

Learn more about Ten Thousand Villages: **http://www.tenthousandvillages.ca/about** and for more on the people who work at Bunyaad see: **http://rugs.tenthousandvillages.com/people_behind_rugs**

Visit these sites for more information about managing forests: **www.us.fsc.org** and **www.ca.fsc.org**

Index